IMPROVISED

How to create the life you really want.

By Robin Konie

PRAISE FOR *IMPROVISED.*

"*Improvised* is the missing piece that so many self-help books miss! Robin takes us on a dance through life with this refreshing outlook on achieving the life you really want. This book is packed with personable and relatable stories that will guide you through a step by step approach to happiness."

~ Halle McCulloch, *Whole Lifestyle Nutrition*

"…. If you're looking for a book that challenges you to breakthrough thinking in your own life from the perspective of a person who has been there, this is a book you'll definitely want to read regularly to inspire and motivate you."

~ Kristen Ethridge, Author, *Harlequin Love Inspired* and Chief Mama at *The Real Time Mama*

".… This is NOT your typical self-help book with lots of rules, to-do lists and goal setting exercises. Conversely, Robin Konie shows you that by letting go of these things and working with the principles of improvisation, a clearer path will be revealed that brings with it more joy, creativity and connection with others."

~ Craig Fear, *Fearless Eating* & Author, *The 30-Day Heartburn Solution*

"Once again, Robin NAILED it! *Improvised* is a beautifully written blueprint that will inspire you to break the chains that are preventing you from living the life of your dreams and propel you into living the one you're destined for. … This book is a must read for anyone who's feeling 'stuck' and not living life to its full potential - personally and professionally."

~ Kristen Boucher, *MIX | wellness solutions for a balanced life* & Creator of *The Superwoman Slim Down*

"I found *Improvised* to be a refreshing change to most 'self-help' books... This is the first self-improvement book I've read that did not stress me out, or make me feel overwhelmed. Reading this book could definitely result in a happier way of life."

~ Stacey Crawford, *Beauty and the Foodie*

"Robin takes goal setting, and living a fun, balanced, happy life to a new level with *Improvised*. This book is unique and energetic. It's both simple and effective. I look forward to having it in my tool box for my clients for years to come!"

~ Melissa Schollaert, Holistic Nutrition Counselor
& Founder of *Real Nutritious Living*

"... As someone who has struggled at times to find joy in the journey, I found *Improvised* to be an inspiring guide to creating the life I want in the present. Improvised showed me how to get to the heart of my desires, how to discover what is driving my dreams and how to create the life I really want while pursuing my goals."

~ Allison Goines, *Our Small Hours*

"*Improvised* offers a playful look into tackling our biggest dreams and taking on the stuff that matters. It delivers a down-to-earth, step by step approach for living from a place of creative purpose..."

~ Julie de Lagarde, *Real Fit Mama* & Author, *Real Fit at Every Age*

"*Improvised* will keep you fully engaged with its analogies and thought provoking stories... I highly recommend this book to anyone searching for their happiness and wanting to create the life they really want!"

~ Kelly Farmer, *The Crunchy Homemaker*

Be sure to download the free companion handbook, "Putting it into Practice" at **www.improvisedbook.com.**

CONTENTS

To my former students and teachers who have shared in the lessons learned from the dance floor.

To my family, for creating beautiful moments in my life every single day.

improvised

INTRODUCTION
the goals we live by

"FORGET GOALS.
Value the process."

JIM BOUTON

LIFE IS LIKE A BOX OF CHOCOLATES … or is it like a bowl of cherries? I've heard life is messy, hard, too short, too long, and everything in between. The truth is we spend a lot of time talking about life and the kind of life we want to live.

The self-help industry is brimming with books and experts aiming to help us achieve that coveted 'dream life' that always seems just out of grasp. We set our eyes on our prize, whether it be a coveted job, the perfect vacation, or the ideal body. Our life's success is measured by numbers, stats, and comparisons. We live by goals, checklists, and vision boards. All of it in the name of reaching our dreams.

I'm not against any of these things. In fact, I've spent many moments of my life writing goals, visualizing the future, and creating many to-do lists to help me realize success.

And yet, there is a problem with all of it. The problem isn't in the intent. We benefit from having hopes, dreams, and actionable items in our life that we set out to realize. The problem lies in the subtle danger of always working for the end result instead of living and creating from the present moment. We are reaching for our dreams, instead of living them. We set our eyes on *the* prize instead of recognizing the other prizes in life that may be even better or right in front of us. We try to control our future by forcing end results that don't consider the complexly-connected nature of life.

Life has a way of pulling us in a lot of directions, which is problematic when you only have one pinpointed target in mind. When we get misplaced, redirected, or stalled, we feel overwhelmed by our inability to stay put on our made-up linear trajectory.

Think about it. How many times did your to-do list get hijacked by something out of your control? The weather, illness, traffic, technology, relationships—there are so many elements, big and small, that help determine the paths of our life.

When we don't realize our goals we blame ourselves: *I wasn't specific enough; I wasn't disciplined enough; my 'why' wasn't big enough.* While those reasons may be part of the issue, I believe the main reason people have a hard time sticking to their goals is that the process is too static. It's too future-only oriented. It's too heavily weighted toward an end result. It reaffirms the myth that we will only be happy when the goal is realized. *When I get that promotion, when I have this much money, when I lose the weight … then I'll be happy.*

Sure, forward thinking is critical to life. I mean, we'd all be in a lot of trouble if we gave no thought to life beyond what's happening right now. But present thinking is just as critical and our approach to goal-setting often forgets that essential point.

Not too long ago, my husband and I were talking about building a home. Not just any home, this was the home we'd been longing for since we were married. Nothing too big, or too extravagant, but a nice home nonetheless: An open floor plan, space for our kids, a kitchen for entertaining, beautiful, clean.

I believed in this home. As I said, I'm a sucker for vision boards, affirmations, and abundant thinking. Business had been doing really well so the timing seemed right. Almost every day I would tell Tom, "We're moving this year into *this* home." We walked through the model home many times, visualizing where we'd put our furniture, what room our kids would sleep in, and so on.

Six months prior to these discussions, any talk about moving into a home like this would have seemed ridiculous, but I have a history of making some pretty 'out there' dreams come true, and I was determined to realize this one.

Not long thereafter, the day came: We put in an offer to the builder for this home.

I remember driving home from the meeting with the realtor. My husband and I were pumped. Another goal met; another check mark on our life's to-do list.

But it didn't happen.

For a number of reasons, both my husband and I felt like the timing wasn't right. A couple days after our initial offer we walked away knowing we'd lose the last lot in the neighborhood. It was the right decision, and I knew it, but a tiny part of me felt crushed. All that planning, affirming and goal setting seemed for naught. I didn't do what I said I would. The visualizations didn't work.

For three days I felt like a failure.

Luckily, common sense kicked in and those moments of feeling like I had let myself down went away. But the lingering feelings left a bad taste in my mouth, not so much because I didn't achieve that big, lofty goal, but because the whole vision of what my future 'needed' seemed so off base.

The problem wasn't that I 'dreamed too big' or didn't work hard enough. The problem was that my dream required too many outside forces to work out, forces I had no control over... And for what reason? To own a piece of property? Is that really my heart's intent?

Of course not.

The whole situation provided some much needed insight that helped me switch up the idea of goal setting. In fact, as I shifted my perspective I realized that my end goal was keeping me from realizing the essence of what I *really* wanted in life. The visions for my dream life were not about a house. The house represented elements of much deeper, foundational dreams. I wanted more space, more freedom, more peace and calm in my life. I wanted to create memories with my family, deepen relationships with friends. I wanted to feel safe and happy.

I let go of the static end goal, partly because it wasn't going to make my life any happier, and partly because I was done forcing an end result at the expense of everything else. Instead, I learned to visualize a life based on intentions or themes for what I wanted: Happiness, peace, space, freedom, and family.

The amazing thing is that this small shift actually gave me a lot more control over the experiences in my life. Why? Because life isn't a choreographed performance. It's an improvisation. If we are only performing for the applause, we've missed the whole purpose of *living*.

When I let go of the physical endpoint (the house) I was open to new possibilities within the real parameters of the life I wanted. Within two months of that experience we were introduced to a beautiful little town that neither my husband nor I had ever been to (or even heard of). While we were there we both felt those things we had been craving: Peace, space, freedom, community. Two weeks later we found an available rental house and moved in.

If we had forced our initial goals to come true we would have missed a deeper, more satisfying experience— a reality we could not have visualized beforehand because we didn't know it existed. I'm so happy we expanded our concept of 'reaching our goals'. Since then we've been applying the principles of improvisation to create the life we *really* want.

That, in a nutshell, is what has propelled this book. Too many people are making the wrong goals, visualizing the wrong things, and basing their success on end results that they may never see and that may not bring them true happiness. All the while they are missing the fun, rewarding improvisation of life.

GETTING STARTED
why improvisation?

"MY WHOLE LIFE has been one big improvisation."

CLINT EASTWOOD

I MAJORED IN DANCE.

That sentence alone will probably create a lot assumptions about me and my life. I don't think anyone was as surprised as I was when I first seriously contemplated the idea of getting a degree in dance. After all, I grew up with the common belief that college is a critical step toward living a happy and secure life. Sure, dance made me happy … but could it also provide security? I mean, dancers aren't generally known for their bank accounts.

In order to convince my overly-rational self (and parents) that I *could* make a career of dance, I made the logical decision of adding a teaching certificate to the plan. Becoming a dance *education* major felt way more secure than *just* a dance major. High school teachers are legitimate. They may not be rolling in the dough, but they have pretty decent job security.

That was the plan.

Feeling good about my decision, I still had to defend my major all the time to my parents, friends, and any random person I'd strike up conversation with:

"You're a dance major? Oh how fun! It must be so nice not to worry about real classes... BUT what are you doing to DO with that major?"

For the first three years my answer was pretty straightforward: "I plan on becoming a high school dance teacher." With a teaching minor in history, surely I had a decent back-up plan if the dance jobs were scarce.

Three years into my major, however, I was having some serious "your gut is talking, listen" moments. Teaching high school just didn't feel right. After all, I have the patience of a two-year-old, so throwing me into a school full of hormonal teenagers seems like a *great* idea, right?

Not really.

After completing almost all the requirements for the education degree, I made the very illogical decision to change my major to 'just' dance. My teachers questioned my decision; my mom questioned my decision; hey, even I questioned my decision. I was back to square one: *What was I going to do with a degree in dance?*

Despite the underlying beliefs that push students to choose 'rational' majors so they can get 'rational' jobs, I felt like my college experience was more than just a preparatory ground for a career. Those four years (plus the two following for graduate school where I received an MFA in modern dance) were a learning haven for me to really get to know myself, my ideals, my weaknesses, and my strengths. I was constantly interacting with interesting people who opened my mind to new ideas and who provided a community that I treasure to this day. I wasn't worried about the job field just yet. With an entrepreneurial mindset, I truly believed that I could make a living *somehow*.

With two not-so-logical dance degrees, I was able to find employment in my field immediately following graduation. The random list of 'other skills' that filled my resume, as a result of the eclectic nature of my schooling, provided other paid experiences through freelance work. I always had a job, and turned down several opportunities throughout the years following graduation.

Was I swimming in the Benjamins? Not even close. But I had a comfortable (dare I say, "secure") life doing something I loved.

More importantly, having the courage to step into a non-traditional major also gave me the courage to leave that career later down the road, even when *that* decision seemed irrational. I now work from home creating a business I love, employing others, and spending time with my husband and two beautiful children. The skills I gained from my major gave me a huge range of experiences to create a truly blessed life.

The funny thing is that, when I talk to other people about their college experiences, I feel like *they* got the short end of the stick, and not just in terms of 'fun', but in terms of meaningful life lessons taught directly from the classroom. In fact, even though I tried to prove my major to others by reminding them about all the 'hard' classes I had to take as a dance major (anatomy, kinesiology, etc.), deep down, the classes that proved to be the most beneficial were the actual *movement* classes, classes like improv.

The foundational principles I learned from improvisation have stayed with me. They have informed my decisions. They have propelled me to take risks and commit to everything I do. The knowledge gained from improvisation has provided me a great deal of security. Granted, that security is not necessarily in the form of traditional job security, but in my ability to adapt and create a good life no matter what comes my way. Life is dynamic, and not enough people know how to live according to the ever-changing nature of it.

To be clear: I'm not suggesting everyone has to major in dance (please, no) or take an improvisation class to live their dreams, but the fundamental 'rules' that I learned in the dance studio are ideas that everyone should know. While they may look slightly different from the angle I present them in this book, they are the same concepts taught through improvisation in the disciplines of theatre and music. The improvisers of the world will appreciate the concepts discussed, but anyone can learn how to apply them to their life in a meaningful way.

The Benefits of Creating an Improvisation Mindset

How many people are living their life as if it was a choreographed performance? We script our conversations, post only the most refined moments of our life for public display, and long for the applause and acceptance of those around us. While we all know the kind of people who seem *totally* rehearsed in their interactions, we generally prefer the genuine 'in the moment' people who listen, respond, adapt, and create a beautiful life seemingly on the fly.

Don't get me wrong, as a dancer I love choreographing and believe there are some powerful lessons to be learned from crafting a work of art. But life is unpredictable, and we need skills to deal with that unpredictability. Enter improvisation.

Students across the world are required to take classes in math, science, and languages … but, as far as I know, there is no general education requirement for improvisation. And that's too bad. Unlike the other lecture-and-regurgitation model classes, improvisation provides real life skills.

Improvisation teaches you:

- How to think critically and creatively
- How to problem solve
- How to work with others
- How to dig deeper
- How to adapt to challenges, changes, and unforeseen circumstances
- How to be brave, open-minded, trusting, and trustworthy

Can you imagine how different our lives would be if we viewed life as such?

- We'd be more respectful of, and learn to honor, ours and other's mistakes.
- We'd live more in the present, being sensitive to the beautiful moments happening all around us.
- We'd have more realistic expectations for ourselves and others.

- We'd know how to better support one another in this journey of life.
- We'd freak out less when things don't go as planned and learn how to adapt to situations with grace.

I could go on, but I think you get the point. Improvisation is a much needed *life skill.*

How to Use this Book

This book is not a 'how to' guide for improvisation. Rather, it's a guidebook for life using some of my favorite principles of improvisation. I've chosen the skills that seem the most neglected or misunderstood in traditional goal-setting books. Before I jump into those skills, it's important that we clarify what I mean and do not mean by the term 'improvisation'.

Improvisation is **not** about being unprepared. It is **not** about 'just winging it', particularly in important situations. Improvisation is **not** about doing whatever you want no matter what.

Improvisation **is** about having a plan while simultaneously being adaptive, responsive, and creative. It **is** about recognizing the synergistic and interconnected nature of life. Improvisation **is** about living with intent. It **is** about taking responsibility for the life we create. Improvisation does take work, practice, and conscious effort.

And yes, improvisation is a lot of fun.

Putting it into Practice

One of the greatest myths about improvisation is that you're either good at it or not. Sure, there are some people with a natural knack for it, but even the masters know that to be really good you have to practice. That's true whether you want to be a master on stage or in life. To that end, I've created a free companion guide to help you put into practice the principles taught in this book. Be sure to grab your free download at www.improvisedbook.com.

Are you ready to create the life you *really* want? Let's begin!

PRINCIPLE ONE
set your intention

"WOULD YOU TELL ME, PLEASE, which way I ought to go from here?" "That depends a good deal on where you want to get to," said the Cat. "I don't much care where," said Alice. "Then it doesn't matter which way you go," said the Cat.

LEWIS CARROLL

Alice's Adventures in Wonderland

I REMEMBER MY FIRST TIME watching a professional comedy improv troupe perform. I was in high school and a handful of friends and I ventured to the city to watch my cousin on stage. With no scripts and a little help from the audience, the performers acted out scene after scene of hilarious dialogue. I don't remember ever laughing so hard.

My initial thoughts about the whole experience bounced back and forth from awe to disbelief. *How could they think so quick on their feet? They never missed a beat! Did they really just make that up on the spot?*

By the time I entered college I had some of my own improv experiences that provided a little more insight. The actors on stage were definitely quick-witted, but they also made sure to set up their improvisations to provide the best odds for success. They designed the games to give all the players the best chance of winning, no matter where the actual dialogue took them.

Likewise, we must consider how we set up our lives. If we just haphazardly move onward we are bound to end up somewhere, but most likely not where we hoped. Life requires a design. If you want to live the life of your dreams you need to make sure you set the stage for success.

Intent is everything.

One of the most fundamental principles I teach as a movement therapist is that the moment of initiation determines the entire outcome. That's true whether you are performing a complex gymnastics phrase or a basic tennis swing. Our neuromuscular system works almost effortlessly when the moment of initiation is programmed with a clear intention. Lack of intent is detrimental to the success of any physical activity and even more so in our lives.

Whether in music, dance, or theater, it is imperative for the artist to know their intent before beginning any sort of improvisational experience. Sure, a true master can 'just fiddle around' and most likely produce something quite lovely, but 'lovely' doesn't necessarily mean coherent. A purposeful performance requires some sort of design to help guide the spontaneity. Is the intent to create new work, develop a theme, prepare for a performance, be entertaining, or something else entirely?

Likewise, our lives unfold with more coherency, grace, and purpose when we have a clear intention to guide us through the weaving and intersecting aspects of our lives. Rather than stumbling on the occasional lovely moments, we see a bigger picture of the unlimited potential within us.

Setting an intention is different than setting a goal. It's a subtle difference, but critical nonetheless. A goal is defined as "the result or achievement toward which effort is directed" (1). It is end oriented, generally with pin-pointed clarity. The best goal setters create steps to help them stay on-track to realize their proposed result. They keep their efforts directed toward the prize while continually defining their 'why' or motivation. Specificity and focus are the name of the game.

An intent, on the other hand, is less focused on one concrete end-result. It is more about purpose and design. It still considers the future and desired outcomes, but it can also be realized right now. It is more open to the entire journey involved.

Let's look at some common goals people set and how they may differ when approached from a perspective of intent:

> Goal: I will lose 20 pounds by my next birthday.
> Intent: I choose to eat healthy, exercise, and focus on quality sleep.
>
> Goal: I want a promotion at work by Christmas.

<u>Intent</u>: I will work hard and am open to opportunities for success.

<u>Goal</u>: I hope to be in a relationship by Valentine's Day.
<u>Intent</u>: I will only surround myself with people I love and who make me feel good.

Now, I know what you're thinking. On the surface the goals may seem better than the intentions. Why? Because every self-help book on the market has indoctrinated us with the idea that we must make concrete, objective goals—numbers, dates, specifics. These are all things we are told we must have in order to achieve results.

I admit, idealistic intentions won't get you very far in life if that's where you start and end. What's the saying? *The pathway to hell is paved with good intentions.* It's true. However, starting with an intention leaves more room for happiness, success, and realization when it's incorporated with the other principles of this book.

Goals vs. Intentions: A Closer Look

Let's say I have a **goal** to lose 20 pounds. We are told that, if we try hard enough and stay committed to our goal, we can make it work. The process seems straightforward: Eat less, exercise more, and only allow for very few 'cheats'.

It works for some, although often only temporarily. But we all know people who do all the 'right' things who still can't seem to make the scale budge. Why? Do they not want it badly enough? Is their 'why' not meaningful enough? Do they just lack discipline?

Keep in mind that I'm not talking about the person who makes a goal to lose 20 pounds and then sits around eating McDonald's all day. I'm thinking of a dear friend who counts every calorie, trains for marathons, and still can't realize her goals. Why? Well, beyond some faulty nutritional advice that continues to perpetuate across America, this is another example of goal setting gone bad.

Despite what those who are trying to sell their diet plans will say, weight issues are very often tied to complex factors that go beyond our discipline to eat less and move more. Often the very element that needs to be changed to realize the goal is the very thing outside of our control.

For instance: Sleep patterns can wreak havoc on our weight loss plans but may be influenced by circumstances we can't change (children, a noisy neighbor, work schedules, etc.). Genetics, autoimmune diseases, hormonal imbalances, adrenal fatigue, or digestive issues may be other hurdles that will keep you from your goal. That's not to say you shouldn't try to lead a healthier life and get to the root issue, it's just that it may take years to identify and heal those things that are causing your weight gain. And in some cases, healing may mean eating *more* and moving *less*. It's not as black and white as the goal masters want you to believe. No wonder so many people feel like failures and give up.

Of course, on the other hand, there are some people who are so bent on reaching their goals that they dip into harmful practices like ridiculous calorie restriction or dangerous weight loss pills, or they ignore all other aspects of their life while obsessing about this one thing. These people *may* be able to realize their desired outcome. But at what cost? Their health? A balanced life? Doesn't that seem counter-intuitive from the original goal?

When the goals don't happen we often revert back to old habits, even if the new habits were really good. We give up, feel defeated, and wait until January 1st rolls by to try again.

A good **intention**, on the other hand, is less concerned with a specific number or the tangible evidence that success was realized. Intentions keep us connected to both the present moment and the future ideal. Focusing on an intention to live healthy instead of worrying about a number on the scale can be a tiny shift in perspective that brings dramatic, lasting results. Being dedicated to healthy living may help you shed those unwanted pounds eventually. It can also boost your energy, improve your skin, and possibly take care of those pesky digestive issues. Your quality of life is bound to improve, and not just in the future when you hit some magic number, *but right now.*

We need to stop pitting our current self and situation with a future ideal that tells us we can't really be happy until our goals are achieved. Instead, let's create intentions that we can live immediately *and* carry with us into the future.

So what does a good intention look like?

It can look like a lot of things. I personally like the idea of themes. Themes help shape the life I want to live. Themes are not tangible, and they are not driven by results that require everything to fall into place for them

28

to be realized. They leave some wiggle room for imperfection. They are *attitudes* and *actions* that I can control *no matter what life throws my way.*

Intentions for your life may revolve around ideas of joy, fun, charity, kindness, success, or hard work. Some of the most fundamental intentions for life include the intent to be:

- Safe, fed, and clothed
- Healthy
- Happy
- Loved

These basic intentions meet our most basic needs and fulfill our human rights. Hopefully, your situation in life provides the necessary factors for them to be realized. If not, they should be your main focus as you work through the principles in this book. If you feel like these basic needs are being met, you can begin to shape your intentions with a more personalized specificity that connects your passions to the dreams for your life. Here are just some possible intentions that you could consider working with:

I have an intention to:

- Travel and meet new people
- Work hard and do my best at work
- Start my own business
- Learn a new talent such as singing, knitting, rock climbing, etc.
- Provide for my family's needs
- Help my children learn and grow
- Become a better conversationalist
- Write a book
- Get more flexible or increase my strength
- Run daily
- Get an education
- Do more service

These intentions are still fairly basic, but there is room for personalization. My own intentions include an intent to move daily, to learn about graphic design, and to help my children explore the world. Be as specific as you need without limiting yourself or getting trapped in circumstances out of your control.

If you have a history of setting goals you don't necessarily need to throw them out the door and start over. We generally set goals because of a deeper desire for our life. Goals for weight loss may be rooted in an intention for healthy living or feeling more loved and accepted. Goals for promotions may stem from intentions for success, recognition, or a desire to do something you love doing. Take a good hard look at your goals and see what the underlying hope is that drives your ambition to realize its reality. Maybe all you need is a shift in your approach. Maybe your goal reveals something missing in your life.

As you create your intentions there are three things to keep in mind:

1. You intention should be something you can control no matter what.

You can't necessarily control the number on the scale, but you can control your habits. This isn't to say that you have to be 100% perfect in those habits, but if your intention requires outside forces to perfectly align it probably needs some adjusting.

2. Your intention should be something you can realize right now.

Again, think attitudes or way of living more than rewards. If you can't start living your intention right now, play around with it until it works for you now as well as in the future.

3. You intention should shape your daily decisions.

Your intentions should push you into action. The best intentions are ones that we can reflect on daily and that serve as a foundation by which we live our lives. If your intentions can only be realized once a year, rethink them.

Ultimately, the main purpose of setting intentions is to provide you with a guiding light that will influence all your decisions. What are the core principles and dreams that you are willing to establish as the home base for your daily living? You are the creator of your own destiny. Your intentions, or lack thereof, will direct everything you do. Set your life up for success and consider your core purpose that will drive you. Take some time to really reflect on the kind of life you want and then create your intentions to make it happen.

ROBIN KONIE

PRINCIPLE TWO
establish parameters

"HAPPINESS IS NOT the absence of problems; it's the ability to deal with them."

STEVE MARABOLI

OH CRAP. I'm stuck.

No, really. I was literally stuck as my body lay glued to the floor, immovable. I was in the middle of an improv that had gone bad. The teacher was a guest instructor and I was beginning to think she really didn't know what she was doing.

Everything started out okay. We began moving with minimal instructions, but gradually more and more restrictions were placed on us.

"You can't use your legs."

"Now you also can't use your right arm."

"Now you have to move with your left hip always connected to the floor."

Each new rule was more difficult and left most of us stuck on the floor, frustrated.

I felt completely unable to move with all the barriers. I had run out of ideas and was mentally done playing this ridiculous game. But something kept me going even though I didn't feel like I was actually dancing, or doing anything for that matter.

Finally, the teacher stopped adding barriers and we were allowed to continue with the many 'cannots' in place. If you think there isn't a lot of potential for dancing when you're forbidden to use your legs, one arm, and are tethered to the floor, you'd be right. We continued in this manner for what seemed like an eternity. It was probably three minutes.

Then something happened. A shift. *A major shift.* It was like a light bulb turned on in a dark, forgotten part of my brain and for the first time in my 20 years of living I saw dance with completely new eyes. My spine became alive as I realized that those 24 vertebrae had more movement potential than my legs with just their two joints. My breath deepened and supported the very full 'dance' that was happening within my torso.

Have I really had this spine this whole time? Why have I never danced with it? Before I knew it, I was engrossed in the exploration of those small but articulate parts of my body that had always played second fiddle to my limbs.

Instead of feeling like I could only make beautiful movement with the defined technique I had been practicing for nearly two decades, I discovered that there was, in fact, a dance to be had even within these confining circumstances. I was totally immersed in the experience and overwhelmed by how much movement potential was available. When the teacher brought the improv to an end I was disappointed not to have more time with this new found freedom.

Bound and Free

The self-help industry generally doesn't talk much about boundaries in a positive light. If anything, we are told we must break through barriers to be truly free. Our brick walls are challenges for us to bulldoze through and conquer. Improvisation, however, teaches us that setting parameters can lead to impressive discoveries. In fact, our barriers are essential to leading a rich life.

A parameter is defined as "a limit or boundary that defines the scope of a particular process or activity" (2). In improv, the parameters could be a myriad of things:

- A spatial barrier: You are only allowed to move in this small 3' x 3' square.
- A physical barrier: You can't use your arms.
- A thematic barrier: You can only dance in curved pathways.

At first glance, these boundaries can be really frustrating. Most dancers I know love to move, but many hate being told *how* to move, especially in an improvisation class. The first couple minutes of the improvisation might be pretty boring as the dancer works with the limitation.

But something magical always happens when parameters are set. As soon as the dancer feels like he has maxed out all the potential movement available within the restrictions placed on him, he soon discovers something new. I see it happen all the time. The committed dancer digs deep and eventually uncovers a well of new ideas. The last half of the improv becomes a fascinating experience as you watch new ideas explode from the boundaries. Parameters force you to think deeper, be creative, and discover options you wouldn't otherwise have considered.

We see this in life all the time.

Think about the woman who learns how to crochet or paint with her feet because she doesn't have physical use of her hands. Think about the blind who walk effortlessly through busy streets even without the use of their eyes. Consider the countless individuals who seem to beat the odds and make meaningful life experiences despite some very hefty restrictions.

Parameters are not placed to cage us. Rather, they provide definition for us to explore our depth as human beings. Whether those parameters come in the form of challenges, upsets, or pre-intended guidelines meant to shape our life, seeing the boundaries helps us realize our own true freedom. That freedom comes in the form of self-expression, personal creation, and depth of character.

Your Personal Parameters

Life will hand you some parameters that are out of your control. You may or may not be able to change them, but looking at them and investigating them will prove useful as you create the life of your dreams. Some of these unchosen parameters may include:

- Physical limitations from illness, injury, or disabilities (or caring for someone with these limitations).
- Your sex, age, and race may create boundaries (whether they should or not is a discussion for another day).
- Environmental factors.
- Choices and actions of others.

No matter how difficult or challenging the barrier may seem, or how unfair the restriction may feel, even parameters that are out of your control provide opportunity to reach deep within your potential and find solutions that people without those barriers will never see. Embrace them as a learning tool; utilize them to create something worthwhile and connect to the world in a whole new way.

Beyond the parameters outside of your control, it is essential to create your own boundaries as you improvise through life. This is where our intentions are given an opportunity to be explored with depth. Say, for example, I have an intention to travel the world. I can create a parameter in my life to help me realize that goal. Maybe that parameter is that I have to spend so many days of the year outside of my home. This parameter forces me to explore new places and realize my intention to travel.

But wait, what if you can't afford to travel? Does your financial barrier trump your designed parameter? Only if you let it. Remember, parameters are intended to make us think critically and search out the answers that are not so obvious. If funds are out of your control that's exactly when you test the parameter. Nobody said you had to travel the world by spending lots of money or taking weeks off from work. Maybe you invest in a tent and try camping in new areas just outside your home. Maybe you ask your boss if you can telecommute for a week each month while you explore neighboring states. Maybe you start by traveling and visiting friends within your own city. Perhaps you start a small online business to create funds especially for traveling. The very idea of what it means to travel can broaden as you explore its depth. If you are willing to dig, be creative, shift your preconceived ideas, and explore *all* the possibilities you'll find that there are a lot of options no matter what boundaries are in your way.

Below is a list of just *some* of the possible parameters you could try on and see what they have to offer. This list is not exhaustive by any means, but hopefully it will get the ball rolling:

- No processed food for 100 days (Intent: Healthy eating)
- No social media sites for a month (Intent: Deepen real-life relationships)
- Try a new recipe each night for dinner (Intent: Improve cooking skills)
- Strike up a conversation with a stranger everyday (Intent: Meet new people)
- Stay away from environments that make me unhappy (Intent: More joy)
- No television at night (Intent: Work on my business)

As you can see, the possibilities are endless. As you begin to consider what type of parameters you might establish to help you realize your intent, consider the following guidelines:

1. Your parameter should provide a challenge.

The whole point of parameters is that they force us to dig deep and uncover untapped potential. They are more than just a rule we live by. As you consider adding a parameter to your life, dare to pick something that is difficult. For example, if you are thinking about a social media parameter to help you deepen real life relationships, limiting your time on Facebook to 20 minutes a day may prove to be beneficial, but it may not provide the actual paradigm shift you need. Rather, swearing off social media entirely for a certain amount of time will prick at the habit you're trying to change.

2. Give your parameter time.

The longer you are willing to sit with the barrier, the more time your mind has to look for new solutions. Again, taking a week off from social media may be really difficult for you. But is that enough time for you to feel free from it? Does it force you to find new methods for relating to others or does it just make you frustrated that you can't connect online? Chances are that a week will be annoying, but not enough time to really let go of the habit and discover something new. Give it a month or two to work past the frustration period and into the "Ah-ha" zone.

There is no exact time allocated for any given parameter, that's up to you. Maybe it's a parameter you want to adopt for life; maybe a month with suffice. Just be sure to make it long enough to provide that space for struggle that leads to ultimate discovery.

Before moving on to the next chapter, take some time to consider how you are setting the stage for your life. Be willing to let go of the goals and embrace larger themes that can guide you as you move within the boundaries you set. Be committed to exploring deeply and staying with it, even when it seems like there are no more solutions. If you're willing to keep at it, the magic will happen. Trust me.

ROBIN KONIE

PRINCIPLE THREE
jump in and play

"PLAY is the highest form of research."

ALBERT EINSTEIN

THE CLASSROM OF 4^(TH) GRADERS sat quietly as they watched the dancers talk about time, space, and energy. The demonstration about the basic elements of dance kept them engaged for the time being. Then the dancers announced that it was the students' turn to move. A handful of young girls squealed in delight. They jumped up and began showing off their favorite ballet steps. But other students were less enthralled by the idea. Several boys sneered that dance was "a girls' thing." Others simply felt anxious about dancing in front of their peers. After all, it wasn't something they had ever done before.

The college dance group that had traveled to this particular elementary school was prepared for the students' mixed feelings about dance. That's why they would not be focusing on steps or technique. Instead they had prepared an improvisation with the intent to make everyone feel comfortable and to get the kids engaged in the process.

Boy, did they get engaged! Freed from the constraints of technical steps, but guided by the parameters given, everyone enjoyed the movement experience. "How many ways can you move your arm? Your leg? Your head?" Before they knew it, the kids were totally invested in creating the most interesting movement they could imagine.

When asked what the students thought about the experience, they all said the same thing: "It was fun!"

The Benefits of Play

Improvisation is one of the greatest examples of play. It doesn't really serve any 'necessary' function. It is generally unrecorded, unscripted, and the physical experience is lost as fast as it was created. As a playful exploration, however, improvisation allows us an opportunity to be childlike. We create, explore, imagine, connect, and enjoy the moment, even though we know the moment will be lost once it's over.

Unfortunately, adults have a huge stigma when it comes to ideas around fun and play. Fun is saved for vacations, weekends, and special events; play is saved for board or video games. We prefer being entertained over true playing. We rarely invest our energy or resources into play as a tool for living out our intentions or building our dreams.

This begs the question: Does play serve a meaningful purpose in our adult lives?

When I watch my daughter play it's clear that she is having a lot of fun. But she's also very serious about her play.

"Mom, you be the queen and I'll be the princess."

"Okay, sounds great, Cami."

"No!!! I'm the princess. Say, 'Okay, PRINCESS'."

Any parent knows that when their children are deep in their pretend scenarios you can't just change it or forget the very detailed scene they've created. It doesn't matter that they just made it up or that they'll probably change who they are within the next two minutes, YOU are not allowed to spoil their imaginative play. And yet, children are also very adaptive and responsive to the world around them. If baby brother shows up, he immediately turns into the royal puppy. If a package is delivered to the house it becomes a treasure chest. The key to their playful imagination is both an **openness** to include whatever comes into their own world and a **commitment** to their interests and passions at that particular moment.

Those sound like important life skills to me, especially when you consider the constantly changing nature of our world. The more open we are to using our imaginations the more resources we have to deal with the unpredictability of life.

50

Sadly, there is not a lot of research available about the importance of play for adults. There is, however, plenty of research about the benefits of play for children. Consider the findings from just one clinical study (3):

- Play allows children to use their creativity while developing their imagination, dexterity, and physical, cognitive, and emotional strength.
- Play is important to healthy brain development. It is through play that children at a very early age engage and interact in the world around them.
- Play allows children to create and explore a world they can master, conquering their fears while practicing adult roles, sometimes in conjunction with other children or adult caregivers.
- As they master their world, play helps children develop new competencies that lead to enhanced confidence and the resiliency they will need to face future challenges.
- Undirected play allows children to learn how to work in groups, to share, to negotiate, to resolve conflicts, and to learn self-advocacy skills.
- When play is allowed to be child driven, children practice decision-making skills, move at their own pace, discover their own areas of interest, and

ultimately engage fully in the passions they wish to pursue.

That's a pretty extensive list of benefits. The study also concluded that we do our children a disservice when we overschedule their days with too many organized activities. Limiting our kids' ability to be self-motivated thinkers by making all their decisions or forcing them into a restrictive schedule can have some far reaching consequences later in life.

What boggles my mind is how we don't see the parallel connections in our own, adult lives.

You need a playcation.

Raise your hand if you feel overscheduled, stressed out, or overwhelmed by everything you need to do.

Chances are you are not alone.

Consider what might happen if we changed our perspective about fun, play, and adulthood. What if we followed the principles of improvisation and looked for ways to have fun *throughout* life and not just in the vacations we take *from* life.

Adulthood is definitely different than childhood. Our concerns are very different. Paying bills, juggling careers, taking care of our homes and family, it all takes time and can be very stressful. Our adult to-do lists can also take a toll on the spontaneous nature of play. We value hard work, expertise, and responsibility. But in my experience play doesn't have to be excluded in order to do real work and fulfill those responsibilities. In fact, it's *because* of all that hard work (and stress that tends to come with it) that we should be making play (and fun) an important part of our lives. When approached in the right way, play can enhance all areas of our adult existence.

An Attitude of Play

So how do we capture this playfulness and incorporate it into our daily life? Simple. Become more childlike.

Okay, so maybe it's not *that* simple. Not in a world that does a pretty good job of taking our natural born tendencies for spontaneity and playfulness and squashing them before we reach maturity. But it is possible. Let's look at some of the ways children interact with their world and see what we can gain from their expertise.

1. Children don't care what other people think.

All you need to do is ask a three-year-old to pick out her clothes. Watch her eyes light up as she launches for her favorite dress-up costume. By the time she's finished she'll be wearing a gold princess dress, cowboy boots, a super-hero cape, one striped sock and one with polka-dots.

Some parents may not let their kids leave the house looking like that, mostly out of concern about what other parents would think about their parenting skills, but little Jenny doesn't care what she looks likes. She feels like Wonder Woman! Nor will her friends care. In fact, they'll be asking their mom why they can't choose their own outfits.

Adults care far too much about what other people think. It's as if we can't shake that junior high school mentality of wanting to fit in. While I'm not suggesting you have to go against all social norms to have fun, I am suggesting that play and fun will be hard to find if you are always worried about others' opinions of you.

I will add: While most kids don't care what others *think* of them, most young children **do** care how other people *feel*. That's an important distinction. It is one of the reasons why they are so adaptive to who they are willing to play with. They know the secret to a good time: Keep your pride checked at the door and follow the golden rule.

2. Children don't have to spend money to have a good time.

I'm not sure when it happens, but somewhere along the timeline of our life we begin to think that fun requires cash. Whether we spend a little (like for a movie ticket) or a lot (big trip to Hawaii), we've lost our ability to find fun that's free. What does free fun even look like?

I was watching my two small children play the other day. One found so much thrill in riding her bike up and down our driveway while pretending she was a racehorse. The other was mindfully examining a pile of rocks, sorting and stacking them. Whether they are playing in nature, dancing to music, climbing trees, or simply using their imagination to create whatever world they want, children are experts at filling their time with fun at no cost to anyone.

Maybe climbing trees isn't your thing, but what about hiking, dancing, painting, photography, visiting a museum, going to a park, singing aloud, running as fast as you can, or having a good conversation with someone you love? There are lots of small and inexpensive ways to bring more fun into our lives if we take some time to ensure that it happens.

3. Children make time for fun.

Sure, it's easy to say that kids don't have the same responsibilities as us, but that doesn't change the fact that they are always making a game out of everything, whether it's a crazy way to eat a sandwich or singing songs while brushing their teeth. Simple tasks become enjoyable because children are always looking for ways to make their world a game. Even Marry Poppins reminds us: "For every job that must be done there is an element of fun. You find the fun and *snap* the job's a game."

There are plenty of moments in even the busiest of days where we can lighten the mood, find the fun, and enjoy the moment. Tell a good joke, skip through the parking lot (remember, you don't care what other people think!), dance while your computer is warming up, even try a game of hide and seek during your lunch break. Why not? Enjoy life a little more.

4. Children are not afraid to make mistakes.

Sir Ken Robinson, in his wildly popular TED Talk, reminds us that children are not afraid to make mistakes. He says:

> "What these things have in common is that kids will take a chance. If they don't know, they'll have a go. Am I right? They're not frightened of being wrong. Now, I don't mean to say that being wrong is the same thing as being creative. What we do know is, if you're not prepared to be wrong, you'll never come up with anything original. And by the time they get to be adults, most kids have lost that capacity" (4).

This ability to give things a try, even in the face of messing up, not only allows children the opportunity to create, it makes their play so much more fun. After all, if we are always afraid of saying the wrong thing, doing the wrong thing, or being the wrong thing, how are we supposed to enjoy life?

This is one of the things I love most about improvisation: It doesn't penalize mistakes. Sure, we like to learn from the moments that don't go as gracefully as planned, but sometimes the 'mistakes' are catalysts for greatness. Embrace your flaws, faults, and blunders.

5. Bored isn't an option.

I know there were plenty of times during my adolescence when I told my mom I was bored, but boredom is actually a state of mind. I remember one high school teacher who explained that only uninteresting people get bored.

To date, I have never heard my daughter tell me she is bored. Sure, she's not even 4 years old, but she is always ready to jump in with a new idea, a new game, or a new way to bring fun into the world. I love her sense of playfulness and pray I can keep harnessing that energy into her later years.

When you find yourself thinking that little phrase, "I'm bored," stop. Just stop. Before you dwell on that feeling, make a list of all the things you could do instead. You get more points if at least one thing on your list is something completely 'just for fun.' You get all the points if you do *that* thing right now.

6. Children follow their passions and interests.

Children play around ideas that ignite their passions. Whether they are interested in bugs, piano, art, or karate, their energy is dedicated to exploring the things that excite them. And when something no longer interests them they are okay moving on to new things.

Can you imagine how different our world would be if adults did the same thing? Sure, not everyone can spend every moment of their life doing what they love. I don't know very many adults who *like* cleaning toilets, paying bills, or washing dishes. But how much of our time is wasted doing things that simply pass time? When I think of the hours wasted on social media (something that generally annoys me more than it gives me pleasure), mindlessly watching television, or some other useless task, I wonder what else I could have done. How could I have fed my passions?

7. Children are willing to jump in.

Very rarely do you have to ask a child twice to jump in and play. If they see another group of kids in the middle of pretend, they are quick to join in. If an idea hits them, they act on it. They live very much in the moment and always err on the side of *doing*.

It can be a lot of fun watching others improvise and perform. That is true in dance, theater, music, and in life. Listening to stories of others doing great things is enjoyable, motivating, and encouraging. Ultimately, however, we will only live the life we want when we are willing to jump in and play along.

Take a moment to think about the kind of stories that inspire you the most. Who are your personal 'celebrities' whom you follow? Are they activists, actors, athletes, politicians, authors, educators? What draws you to them? Is there something about their life that you'd like to see in your own?

What do you feel is holding you back from experiencing the same kind of enjoyment they seem to have? I'm not suggesting that everyone will be able to be the next Hollywood celebrity or business mogul, but I'm also not suggesting that you can't. Even though your life will look very different from that of *anyone* else you admire, there is plenty of room for everyone to jump in and make the most of the life they have.

The physical experience of play may be lost as soon as it is created, but the lessons learned can stay with you forever. Make a commitment to add more play to your life. Your life can be fun *and* rewarding. You can do a great work *and* play. Start seeing your life from a child's perspective. Look for the moments where you can indulge in the spontaneous, jump in the fun, and bask in the very important life lessons offered through it all.

PRINCIPLE FOUR
suspend judgment

"PEOPLE HASTEN to judge in order not to be judged themselves."

ALBERT CAMUS
The Fall

MY FIRST REAL EXPERIENCE with improvisation as a dancer was, unfortunately, anything but pleasant.

The day started early as 13 students and I marched, foggy-eyed, into the small conference room. We were each representing our school as a Sterling Scholar. The Sterling Scholar program recognizes and awards high school seniors for the pursuit of excellence in scholarship, leadership, and citizenship in the State of Utah. Potential candidates create portfolios to display their work in a specific category and go through a series of interviews at high school, regional, and state levels (5).

These early morning meetings weren't too bad as more than half of the other scholars were some of my best friends. The meetings were designed to prepare us for the regional interviews coming up. Watching your peers answer practice questions in their chosen category is fun. It's not often you get to witness your high school friends really claim their passions.

As the Dance Sterling Scholar I really didn't know what kind of questions to expect for my practice interview. Maybe I'd be asked something about the creative process or the value of arts in education? My mind was already preparing answers before it was even my turn.

The school counselor who was running these preschool meetings asked me to come to the front of the room. Confused by the request, as everyone else was allowed to answer their questions sitting in their seats, I walked up next to her. The conference room was quite small. With one large table that could seat all 14 of us, there was little room left for anything else. I looked back at my friends who were laughing silently at my discomfort. *Thanks, guys.*

Then it happened. The counselor looked me in the eyes and very firmly said, "I want you to dance 'anxiety'."

Excuse me?

Anxiety. Just dance anxiety? No other instructions? No preparation? Nothing. I felt my heart begin to race. My mind was calculating all the reasons I couldn't do what she asked: *You don't just dance anxiety! What a stupid idea. There's not nearly enough space in here to dance. I can't do it. Why would I make a fool of myself in front of these other people who know nothing about dance? There's no way I can do what she wants. I'm not dressed appropriately to dance well. Did I mention there's not enough space? No. This is really, REALLY stupid.*

The judgments were practically shooting out from my mind in fiery darts of glaring annoyance toward this woman. I couldn't seem to stop the constant "no" that kept swimming up in my throat from deep within my gut. *No. I do not want to do this. Not now. Not here. Not ever.*

So what did I do? I'm not really sure. I mean, my gut was saying "no" but my body did *something*. I moved, very awkwardly. Like, *really* awkwardly. My red face matched the anger and shame I felt in those brief few moments that seemed to last forever. My friends 'lovingly' mocked the experience, not realizing how upset I was over the whole situation. When it was over I sat down in my chair, ready to go home.

Did this woman know how to guide an improv? No. There was no real set up, no parameters, nothing to make me feel committed or safe in the experience. In her defense, though, she was doing what she thought would help me prepare, even if she didn't do it very well.

Fast forward 5 or so years and that experience would come back to haunt me. Not so much because of how embarrassed I felt at the time, but because of how adamantly I shut down the possibility of success. Instead of opening up to the idea that I could dance with a theme of anxiety, I let my own literal anxiety and quick judgment keep me from even trying. All I could think of in that moment was the millions of excuses why the assignment was stupid. Had I been willing to suspend my judgment for even a minute, who knows? Maybe I could have created something really meaningful.

Judge Not.

Some students say that you should have no judgment while improvising. Anything goes. There are no rules, no right or wrong. "Be completely free," they say. True, there are some instances where that may be the intent of the movement experience. Heaven knows we need some moments like that in our life. "Come. Move. Play. Explore your possibilities, and don't worry about a polished end result." Needless to say, the safe environment provided in the studio during those improv classes was a much needed retreat for many.

More often than not, however, the true principle behind improvisation isn't one of *no* judgment. It's one of *suspended* judgment. The difference between the two ideas is critically important.

Nobody likes to feel judged, especially if we feel we have been judged rashly. But we do it all the time. It is part of our natural instinct and it can serve us in extreme situations that require us to think quickly on our feet in the face of possible danger. But most of our life is not caught up in those intense situations, thankfully, which means we could all benefit from learning how to suspend judgment more often.

In improvisation, suspending judgment means staying with something long enough to really see what it's about. Maybe there is a parameter that an actor can only speak the same three words throughout the entire scene. Maybe his initial judgment is that it won't be funny or the audience won't like it. His judgment is telling him to stop and save the scene, or at the very least, his dignity.

But improvisation asks us to suspend our judgment for a bit. Sure, only saying the same three words would be ridiculous in real life, but what might it do in a comedy scenario? The rule of suspended judgment says, "Let's try. Stay with it a little longer before making any final decisions."

Judging the Real Life

In living out the life of our dreams, the principle of suspended judgment can be extremely beneficial as it gives us some breathing space to try new things. Of course, I'm not talking about moral aspects like killing, robbery, bullying, etc. These things will always be wrong and should require no time to just say "no." Rather, I'm talking about the choices that have the potential to bring us closer to (or further away from) our intentions for the life we want.

If I have an intention to start my own business, I may feel a push to quit my job so I can dedicate more time to my work. If I am too quick to judge I might choose to hand my boss a letter of resignation before the day is over. Mission accomplished! Of course, 24 hours later I'm ready to have a heart attack as I realize I have no money to pay the bills and I am months away from earning any income from my new endeavor.

In a reverse scenario, a moment of rash judgment could bring a completely different result. Say you have a moment of wanting to quit your job but quickly remind yourself that you'd have no money and no way to support yourself. You not only talk yourself out of leaving your current position, but you convince yourself that you'll never be ready to leave. You may have missed out on the heart attack, but you've also just killed your dreams of being a business owner.

When you suspend judgment you allow yourself some time to just be with an idea. Maybe the thought comes to you: *I want to quit my job*. Rather than jumping into a dialogue of why that would be amazing or awful, you just let the feeling sit. You recognize it, but don't act on it. You don't attach any preconceived idea to it.

You wait for the thought to come again, acknowledge it, and continue sitting with it. You let it work in your mind. Maybe by the third time the thought crosses your mind you feel prepared to dig a little deeper and pull the possibilities apart. In that space you explore some options for extra income that could keep you afloat while you get things started. In that space you detail some ideas that would ensure you're ready to launch your business in a timely manner. In suspending your judgment you decide *when* you should quit your job instead of deciding now or never.

A lot happens in the waiting, and it isn't always easy. Just ask my husband. I tend to be a "let's just do it" type of gal. If an idea comes to me I like to jump on it like a cat on a field mouse. Tom is the opposite. When an idea hits him he will let it simmer for weeks, months, years if needed. His never-ending patience requires a lot of patience on my part! But it has also taught me a lot of important lessons about suspending my need to act now.

That's not to say there aren't times when you should act now. There will be decisions in your life that demand a quick answer, but I find that the practice of suspending judgment is still valid. If the situation warrants a more rushed response, the compulsion to act usually keeps coming. I may suspend judgment but it is only seconds before I feel the push again. I don't sit with the idea for very long, but I still give it a moment to confirm its need for response.

Turn Away from the Mirrors

Look in the mirror and what do you see? For many of us the response is a rash judgment about our inability to meet the ideals of society. Ask any dance teacher and they will tell you about their love/hate relationship with mirrors. Mirrors can be a useful tool to help students see what's going on with their body, but mirrors can also be very misleading. They have a tendency to force students to rely on visual feedback instead of learning how to listen to and master the body from the inside out.

Most improvisation classes will utilize a 'no mirror' rule. Improvisation is less about what things look like on the outside. Contact improvisation, for example, is a wonderful practice that utilizes the laws of physics and points of contact (contact with the floor, with a partner, or even a group) to create some beautifully complex movement. If you rely on mirrors while trying to participate in a contact improv you are destined to get injured. Too many rash judgments are made from worrying about what is seen in the mirror.

Consider the 'mirrors' that distract us from feeling what's really happening from the inside out. What things distort our reality and make it difficult to honestly judge or assess a situation or person? Social media, peer pressure, the news and media outlets: All of them provide selected pictures of the lives around us and we tend to compare our reality with what is presented. Never mind that we are comparing our real-time experiences with everyone's carefully selected highlights. We make decisions on health, fashion, education, and even career choices based on what we hear and see in the outside world, even if it's not a true reflection of our own values for our life.

The more space we give ourselves to think through big decisions (or even small decisions) the more opportunity we have to turn inward and ensure that our judgment is coming from an authentic place and not one reflected off of the mirrors of society. Turning away from these mirrors of life can be a simple tool for practicing the art of suspending judgment.

"Yes, and…"

This is one of my favorite practices for learning how to suspend judgment. As an important practice in theatrical improvisation, the rule behind "yes, and..." is that you never say "no" to your improvisation partner.

> In Tina Fey's bestselling book, *Bossypants*, she outlines the rules of improv: Always say "YES, AND..." meaning, always agree, and add something to the discussion. For example, in an improvised scene with a partner, never say no. If you're in a boat rowing down the river, you don't say, "No, we're folding laundry." You say, "Yes, and we could really use a paddle instead of my arm." It adds to the scene, humor can develop, and trust is established between scene partners (6).

This practice can also help us suspend judgment. Too many are too quick to say "no," especially if the situation questions the status quo. Consider some of the everyday possibilities that we very casually push aside and what might happen if we suspend judgment and open up to the possibility of "yes."

> *Should I quit my job and become a professional blogger?* (Gut reaction: No way!) **Yes, and** I'll be ready to do it when I make at least 80% of my current salary from blogging.

Can I take a year off and travel the world? (Gut reaction: In your dreams.) **Yes, and** I'll do some research on how telecommuting will save my company lots of money and present the idea to my boss.

Should I sign up for that yoga class I've been researching even though I can't touch my toes? (Gut reaction: It will be less awkward if I just stick to a DVD.) **Yes, and** I'll see if Becky wants to join me. We can be beginners together!

It's difficult to even imagine all the times we immediately shut down ideas for our dream life. The little voice in our head is so good at quickly rejecting any thought that rocks the boat too much. That is our tendency toward judging too quickly. Start paying attention to the negative talk and then just try saying "yes, and" and see where it goes.

Suspending judgment is one of the trickier principles of improvisation because making quick judgments comes so naturally. Most of us aren't even aware that it's happening. Finding small ways to bring attention to that initial moment of judgment, even if we have to start with the small and seemingly insignificant ideas, can make a world of difference as we open up the possibilities of our life beyond our current imagination.

PRINCIPLE FIVE
commit to risk

"A SHIP IS SAFE in harbor,
but that's not what ships are for."

WILLIAM G.T. SHEDD

A FEW YEARS AGO my younger brother and some friends started an improv comedy troupe called "...And Go!" I was there for their inaugural performance. The team of friends had reserved some space in a local church auditorium. It was a free show and the audience members were either related to or close friends of the performers. This first performance was full of funny, well-played moments. And, as was to be expected, there were several moments that fell flat.

I remember driving home with my husband discussing what we had seen, what we loved, what needed work, etc. We're not theater critics by any stretch of the imagination, but we enjoy analyzing performances since both of us have spent a lot of time on stage. Without much thought, we both immediately identified which performers we thought did the best job. *But what made them stand out?* That was less obvious.

Over the next few months, as we continued to show up for the free performances, I began sifting out the things that made certain players more enjoyable to watch. There were a lot of differences in the style of comedy from one performer to another: Some were more outrageously silly, others more dry in their humor, some more fast-paced. But the one thing that all of the 'good' actors had in common was a **commitment** to whatever they were doing and a willingness to **risk** in their performance.

(For the record, "...And Go!" went on to land a gig in a locally owned old movie theater and became true professional improvisers with a paying audience. Pretty cool, right?)

Make the Commitment

In life, we commit to a lot of things. We commit to sticking with a particular phone carrier for two years. We commit to taking out the garbage for pick-up once a week. We commit to keep cats fed. On a much deeper and more 'committed' level, we commit to relationships, families, faiths, values, and (hopefully) ourselves.

Unfortunately, too many people confuse the idea of commitment with the idea of bondage. We think we are shrugging off our responsibility if we leave the job we hate or stay in an abusive relationship. Some people play the martyr in the name of commitment to stay in something they know is not feeding their lives because of guilt, fear, or shame.

Commitment is not the same thing as staying trapped in a dead-end situation.

Rather, commitment should be connected to those intentions we have set for our life. I am committed to hard work, but I am not committed to a company that treats me poorly. I am committed to loving relationships, but I am not committed to settling for cheap experiences that ultimately leave me feeling more alone. I am committed to healthy living, but I am not committed to dangerous diets or harmful workouts. I am committed to happiness, but I am not committed to quick substitutions that don't last.

When we stay stuck in a place that doesn't serve us or the other people involved, we are actually using the idea of commitment to cover up the real issue: *A fear of risk.*

Sarah Addison Allen said, "Happiness is a risk. If you're not a little scared, then you're not doing it right." I dare say that there are a lot of people not doing it right. How many of us are truly committed to taking the risks that can change everything for the better?

What risks are we talking about? Well, in improvisation the most commonly discussed risks include:

- The risk of looking stupid
- The risk of falling or getting hurt
- The risk of doing something 'wrong'

Look familiar? We face some of the same fears in life that performers do on stage. Nobody wants to look stupid, get hurt, or do something wrong. But risks in life can seem a lot more daunting than risks on stage because, when all is said and done, improv is still just a kind of game. Risks in life have more far-reaching consequences if they don't work out.

Are there risks not worth taking? Of course. You don't need to risk your life to prove you're brave enough to jump off a ridiculous height. You don't need to risk your health by trying to compete with the guy next to you at the gym. You don't need to risk your marriage by quitting your job without discussing it with your spouse. To be clear: Risking is not the same thing as being careless or selfish.

If you're not sure if the risk is worth taking, consider looking at it through the principles of this book.

Ask yourself:

- Does this risk help me stay in line with my intentions for life?
- Does the risk keep me within the parameters I've set?
- Does the risk bring more fun and opportunities for play?

- Am I making a rash judgment by risking?
- Does the risk keep me committed to values I believe in?
- What could I gain from risking? What could I lose?

How does the risk add up when you answer those questions? Is it something that brings you closer to or further away from the life you *really* want to live?

My Moment of Risk

A few years ago I came across an old box full of various photos, keepsakes, and other random pieces from my childhood. Among the treasures was a single worksheet from the 3rd grade. It was one of those questionnaires that most children fill out at least a half dozen times during their first ten or so years of life. This particular document was filled out by my 8-year-old self.

The questionnaire had your typical questions: What is your favorite color? Favorite food? Best friend? Etc. I had a good laugh as I read through some of my answers. I learned that I didn't like pork chops, I loved the color yellow, and my spelling was really, really bad. Like really, bad. But then I came across that most important question: **What do you want to be when you grow up?**

Isn't that *the* question when you are little? Let's be honest, it's *the* question when you start high school, apply for college, upon graduation, and onward.

The question is pretty magical when you're 8 because the sky's the limit. At 8 you can be an astronaut, the President of the United States, or a movie star. At 8 most people don't tell you that your dreams for your adult life are ridiculous, unlikely, or made-up.

So you can imagine my surprise when I glanced over my 8-year-old answer. What did I want to be when I grew up? A dance teacher. (Technically, I wrote "dace" teacher... See, bad spelling.)

I remember sitting there gazing at the yellow paper with my barely legible handwriting. A dance teacher. I was surprised by the whirlwind of emotions that came up as I stared at my response. Why didn't I pick something more, I don't know, more ... exciting? Where was my imagination? Where was my big dream? Where was the magic?

At the same time I felt a sense of pride and accomplishment. After all, I was a dance teacher. Despite all the naysayers and good-intentioned-but-not-so-motivating folks who told me that majoring in dance was a waste of time, I had successfully danced through many years of school to land a job as a dance professor at the university with the largest dance program in the world.

I had apparently realized my 8-year-old dream. I answered the question right. I made a plan and stuck to it. I became a dance teacher.

Kudos to me.

And yet, it was at this exact same moment that I began to feel a gnawing feeling in my gut. Despite the fact that I enjoyed dance, loved teaching, and felt pretty darn good about my skills at my chosen profession I was also beginning to feel the seeds of change planting roots in my heart. The scary thought crept from the back of my mind and stood boldly in the forefront: **I didn't want to be a dance teacher.**

It was an odd realization because I didn't hate what I was doing, but I didn't love it either. At one time I did. At one time teaching dance was an absolute joy. I remember coming home and telling my family, "I can't believe they pay me to do this!" During those years I felt enlivened by my job. I was deep in passion, and that passion gave me life lessons and opportunities to grow and learn. That passion helped me instill passion in my students. It was wonderful.

But those days began to fade. Now I only *liked* what I did… I no longer loved it. And then I realized that, if I wanted to keep growing, learning, serving, and feeling fed by life, I needed to make a change. Why? Because I was committed to the intention to live a life doing what I love. That doesn't mean I love 100% of what I do 100% of the time. That's not really realistic. But there needed to be more passion than what was there. Because, as a teacher, I knew my students needed that passion, too. If I didn't love what I was doing it wasn't just affecting my life, it was affecting theirs.

But quitting was scary. I mean ... hadn't I *always* wanted to be a dance teacher? Didn't I spend years and loads of money to get to this point? I continued to teach for a couple years (suspending judgment at its finest), and during that time an interesting thing happened. I had probably a dozen students approach me seeking advice. One by one, in almost the same exact language, these twenty-somethings confided their insecurities about their own future. "Robin," they would say, "I still don't know what I want to do with my life."

Some of these students were seniors, ready to graduate, others were freshmen looking to choose a major. I heard many of the same concerns whispered in my office: "Can I make a living as a dancer?" "My mom thinks I should major in something else." "I just don't love what I do anymore, but only have one semester left... I can't change my major now, can I?"

My response to them was pretty much the same: "I have spent my life working to get the job I now have, and I still don't know what I want to do with my life. I still can't say for sure what I'm going to be when I grow up."

We live in a world that pressures us to make decisions about our life's path early on. We ask our children what they want to be when they grow up without realizing what the most obvious answer should be: **I want to be happy**.

Teaching dance made me really happy. And then it didn't. So I risked it all and I quit. I left a job that many wanted. I left coworkers who I loved. I left students who I adored. I left a profession that I had literally spent most of my life preparing to enter. I left because I was committed to happiness more than a job, happiness for me and for the people I interact with. I honestly believe you can't have one without the other.

And you know what? It was an amazing decision. It was not an easy one ... not even close. In fact, my mother was very vocal about her concern and the risks involved. I left a secure job with secure benefits at a time when my husband was not employed. I left at a time when the economy was in the dumps. I left at a time when we were talking about starting a family. I left without a real plan for what I was going to do next. I left not knowing if I was making a mistake, but confident that if I didn't try something new I would regret it for the rest of my life.

Things did work out through hard work, faith, and some uncomfortable times. I found a new niche that fueled a passion my 8-year-old self didn't even know existed. I met new people. I learned new things. I was riding the waves of joy again. I was fulfilled by new experiences and, in return, felt like I was contributing to the world in a positive way.

The best part? I know that this new place isn't a permanent one. Life is not scripted, it is improvised. I'm not afraid of changing again. I have the courage to switch plans a dozen or more times if needed. I no longer feel pressured about picking a single career or path. Life is not etched in stone. I am committed to the intentions for this life, and willing to risk some comfort to get there. I want to be happy. That is my firm plan. Everything else is up for grabs.

Motivation for the Risks of Life

I don't know your story. I don't know what risks are staring you in the face. I don't know what specific intentions you are holding for your life. But I do know that you probably want to feel happy, loved, and successful, because we all do. When risking seems too hard, consider the following:

Very little in life is permanent. If you make a mistake, good for you! Learn from it and move on. I promise it won't be your last mistake, but you will be stronger and smarter for it.

Consider what you have to lose. In most instances it's not very much. Even in the face of those 'big' moments of our life (careers, relationships, home) if everything were to go wrong there is still room for much happiness.

Always remember what you have to gain. A job you enjoy, a happy marriage, freedom to travel the world, new friends, success, abundance, opportunities! There are so many things waiting for you if you are willing to take the risks and *enjoy the ride.*

Make the jump. Suspend judgment and open up to the possibility of fun. With the right parameters and intentions, you can stay within the purpose of your life while opening up the potential for greatness.

ROBIN KONIE

PRINCIPLE SIX
be present

"THE BEAUTY of this day doesn't depend on its lasting forever."

MARTY RUBIN

THE CLASS STARTED OUT like any other morning technique class. The day was gray and looming with the threat of a blistery winter storm. I stood looking out the window down below at the students who were racing to get to their morning classes. I turned around and took in the room I had grown to love. The dance studios at the University of Utah are beautiful—high ceilings, lots of windows, natural light, and my favorite thing: Space to move in.

The teacher, Eric, walked in and began class as he normally did, with an improvisation. The purpose of this morning ritual was mostly aimed to warm up our bodies and prepare our minds. Eric began guiding us through that day's experience. "Feel what parts of your body are connecting to the floor. Roll away from those points. Notice what parts of your body are now contacting the floor. Roll away." My joints were becoming more fluid as I sighed deeply into my breath.

I love moving.

We continued exploring and improvising in this same manner for a couple of minutes and then Eric just let the dance grow organically where it wanted to go. That day, the class seemed magnetized to one another as a group contact improvisation began to take shape.

Contact improvisation is not necessarily about performing (although it can be pretty amazing to watch). It's about physics. It's about using the parameters of our own bodies and their relationships to gravity and points of contact. My foot on the floor: Point of contact. My hand on someone's arm: Point of contact. My hip balancing on someone's back: Point of contact.

During those first few months of graduate school I actually had a love/hate relationship with contact improvisation. I loved watching it. I loved seeing the almost acrobatic movements that grew from the group. I loved moving with so many talented dancers. But I also feared it because I was not used to giving my weight to other people. There is a lot of trust that goes on in contact improvisation and I apparently had some trust issues.

In this particular experience I found myself doing what I unfortunately tend to do in all areas of my life: Plan ahead.

This just doesn't work in contact improvisation, you **have** to be fully present in the here and now. But I was trying to second guess the move of everyone who crossed my path. It made for some awkward connections to say the least.

And then I met up with *him*. He was an undergraduate student, so I didn't know him well, but I was aware that he loved contact improv, especially weight bearing, lifting, and all that cool-but-kind-of-freaky-toss-you-in-the-air-while-I-balance-on-this-dancer's-ear stuff. You know, the kind of stuff I liked to avoid. To make matters worse, this guy was **teeny.** Seriously, he was five foot nothing and skin and bones. I was 5' 6" with some nice 'meat' to my frame. I did NOT want to improvise with this man.

But you don't just walk away from a group improv. You just don't. Especially not in graduate school. I had nothing against this dancer, he was extremely kind, talented, and capable. I just had my own insecurities about my abilities and body.

In those brief seconds I started plotting out my evasive maneuvers to avoid connecting with him. I shut down any real opportunities for partnering with the dancers in the room and zoned in on my own life, focusing on past experiences and future fears that stalled my ability to be fully present in the moment. I was determined not to relate with anyone for the next few minutes.

It failed. Wonderfully.

This dancer was fully present. He was also incredibly skilled and understood physics in an astonishing, kinesthetic way. Before I had a chance to think too far into the future I was sky bound. I have no idea how it happened, but for thirty or so seconds I suspended judgment and let what happen just happen.

It felt like a dream. I remember at one moment looking at my reflection in the mirror and wondering how I could be so high off the ground. This dancer took that moment and somehow connected with other dancers and before I knew it I was being passed around like some fanatic hipster in a mosh pit. Except instead of fanatic, it was graceful, surreal, and absolutely breathtaking.

By the time my feet touched the ground I was completely changed. My sabotaging beliefs about my abilities and those around me shifted. I was finally connected to the community of dancers, and more willing to risk and commit. Those thirty seconds still spark in my mind from time to time. It was a moment of pure bliss as I lived fully in the present.

The Gift of Being Present

Remembering and learning from our past is essential to living. Likewise, if we didn't consider our future intentions we'd be aimlessly walking around this life with no direction or purpose. But what about the present? Many people are *living* in the present without *being* in the present. In fact, our society's inability to be truly present is one of the most challenging realities of our over-stimulated world.

Being present is being open to the world, situations, and people around us. Not just *in* the world, but available *to* the world. It's about how we give our attention and who we gift it to.

We live in very unique times. Never before in the history of the world have people had so many opportunities for distraction. IPods, smartphones, and tablets allow us to tap into a virtual world of information that people 20 years ago couldn't even imagine. While the benefits and convenience of these gadgets are many, they also diminish our ability to be truly present.

In a chilling photo essay, London-based photographer Babycakes Romero created a photography series of non-staged images featuring people obsessed with their smartphones. (You can see the images here: http://bit.ly/dealthofconv).

Each picture tells a sad tale of missed opportunities for relationships and interaction. The images of a couple out for dinner, friends at a social event, and co-workers on the job, each sucked into their own digital reality without giving anything of their own self to the world around them.

In Romero's own words:

"I started to photograph people in company on their phones as there was a certain symmetry to them and it appealed on a visual level, but as I continued I noticed an inherent sadness to the proceedings.

"Before mobile phones were invented, people would have had no choice but to interact. However, that is no longer necessary as we can all now 'pretend' we are doing something 'important' on our devices rather than think of something to say. This is killing conversation. I believe it's increasing social pain" (7).

Of course, smartphones are not the only tool we can use to withdraw from the moment. Have you ever found yourself not listening to a friend because you were lost in your to-do list? Have you ever nodded your head to appear engaged while watching the television screen mounted on the wall in the restaurant? Have you ever held back your feelings because you are dwelling on past mistakes or fears? Have you ever played a completely made-up conversation in your head that never took place?

Our lives are full of things that can pull our attention away from the here and now. In the process we find ourselves socially isolated and simultaneously longing to be loved and understood.

Of Critical Importance

Why does any of this matter? Because life is all about connections. *We* are all connected. Living your dreams requires you to recognize your relationships within the world. Remember, no man is an island. So why do we approach our goals as if we are the only factor in making them happen?

Goal setting propels us into 'future' mode. It forgets the importance of being present. Our lives are not isolated from the world and the people we live with. To try to force a future we desire without being open to the experiences and people around us *right now* is foolish and ultimately fruitless. Besides, if we are only concerned with our own life and reality, we are missing the fun and meaningful relationships that make life worthwhile.

So how can we practice being more present? For starters, we need to notice our habits for disengaging. As I mentioned, I have a major tendency to jump into the future and start planning events. There are times when that serves me, and there are times when I miss out on some beautiful experiences happening around me right now. I have noticed I also tend to disconnect when I feel overly busy. Because I'm the type of gal who loves to get things done in a timely manner, if my to-do list is too overbooked I have a hard time being fully present as I am always trying to battle the 'should be done's' in my head.

The other times I commonly skip out of the moment are when I feel bored. I already talked about the nature of boredom. *Yes, apparently I am an uninteresting person.* Yet I've noticed that the 'boredom' I generally experience is a direct result of being too tapped into social media. As a blogger, social media is really more about business to me than it is about socializing. But the nature of the beast is one of distractions. Sure, I log on to do some work, but before I know it I've been sucked into whatever 'stuff' is selected for my newsfeed. Some of it is interesting; some of it is totally stupid. But it feeds part of my brain that now feels it needs to be constantly entertained.

How many times do you check your computer or app to see if anything interesting has been posted? I found that, for myself, any time there is a tiny lull in the day I automatically grab my phone to just 'check in'. It was only after some conscious effort that I realized all that 'checking in' was actually forcing me to check out of the real life happening around me.

Not wanting to miss any more of the life around me I finally said, "Enough is enough," and removed the app from my phone. I'm not suggesting you have to give up Facebook or Instagram or whatever happens to be your particular weakness, but maybe making it less accessible might help you overcome the temptation to always disconnect from life.

Beyond the Distractions

Once the distractions are removed, or at least lessened, there is still a practice to being present. Things like daily meditation and breathing exercises can be great tools to help you learn how to be more in the moment. If you are completely new to the idea, here are the three steps I like to practice:

1. I notice everything around me. When my mind starts to disengage, I stop and take in my environment. I notice *everything*. Who is in the room? What are they doing? What are they wearing? What color is the paint on the walls? What is the floor like? What is the temperature? What sounds do I hear? What can I smell?

I run through this list quickly and I don't dwell on anything. Dwelling usually spins my thoughts into a whole new tangent. Instead, I take in the very objective elements of my world. I open my eyes and simply *notice*.

2. I notice how I feel in the moment. This is not the time for me to analyze deep emotional feelings. Instead, I simply take stock of where I am *right now*. Do I feel hot or cold? Do I feel my feet on the floor? Am I hungry? Thirsty? Do I feel tired or energized?

3. I try to see the world from someone else's perspective. Depending on the situation this may be as simple as changing where I am standing to literally see their perspective, or it might be as complex as trying to understand a tiny part of the world from their point of view. If we are conversing, this is where I will spend my energy until we are done. I will listen intently. I will try to feel what they are feeling. I will try to understand what they are saying and experience it fully with them.

Honestly, I'm not very good at this third part, but I am practicing. It's amazing what the true art of listening can do for a relationship. It's also amazing what you can learn and incorporate in your own life.

Being Present With Yourself

Learning some tips and tricks to help you be more aware and engaged with others is a great way to practice the art of being present. There is also need, however, to practice being present with ourselves. Being present is about the *being* aspect of living. That can be difficult in our world that puts a lot of value of the doingness of life. *What did you do today? What are you going to do when you grow up? What have you done with your life?* If you tell your spouse that you spent your day sitting in a grassy field just *being*, they may think you're crazy *and* that you wasted your day.

But taking time to practice being mindful and open to the many possibilities of life is essential in creating a life you love. Not only are there incredible health benefits from taking time to stop *doing* every now and then, but you'll find you'll never really deeply practice the other elements of the improvised life if you don't give some space to engage with it on a personal level.

So how do you practice being present with yourself? I actually like to follow the same three steps listed above with a slight tweak to the last one:

I start by taking myself out of past or future thinking and simply take in the world around me. What sights, sounds, or scents do I sense? Then I think about the things I'm feeling. The temperature, the points of contact with the earth, my posture, my breath, etc.

Finally I try to see the world with new eyes. Since I'm not with anyone during this practice this is less about seeing someone else's perspective and more about opening my thoughts to new ideas. Without fail my mind will wander and I'll start to get carried off in my to-do list for the day, past memories, or future plans. As soon as this happens I try to pull myself back into the present and focus on my breath: Inhale, exhale, inhale, and exhale.

For those who love concrete activities and actionable to-do lists this practice will seem really hard or even completely ridiculous. I'd like to propose that those who feel this way are precisely the people who need to spend more time in this meditative, open state.

Our goal isn't to spend our entire existence in this non-doingness. After all, there are plenty of things we need to do that are worth doing well. But the more we practice the art of being, the more easily we can access it when the time warrants. We can be more empathetic listeners, more observant travelers, and more open to the wonderful and unexpected opportunities that are coming into our lives that far too many people miss because they are sucked into a reality that leaves no room for spontaneity.

ROBIN KONIE

PRINCIPLE SEVEN
Find your community

"EVERY PERSON is defined by the communities she belongs to."

ORSON SCOTT CARD

THE LOOK ON THEIR FACES said it all. There was not a lot of faith that the experiment would turn out well. I was prepared for this. After all, I had given the same 'assignment' to other classes, and each time the same look of anxiousness and uncertainty bubbled to the surface.

"Let's go over the rules one more time," I suggested, trying to calm the dancers' fears. "When the music starts you begin moving. Move however you want. Move to warm up your body. Move to feel beautiful. Move to get out excess energy. It doesn't matter how … just move."

Everyone sighed a little as I went through the first set of instructions. Telling a dance major to dance is a no brainer. It's the second set of instructions that always gets them.

"Then, when the moment feels right, someone, anyone, can yell out 'ME!' Make it loud and clear so everyone can hear you. After you yell 'ME', start giving into gravity, or, in other words: Fall. Think of it as a suspended fall, but do be willing to go all the way down. When the rest of us hear someone yell, it is our responsibility to rush to them. As a class we will lift that person up before they hit the ground. We'll move them to a new place in the studio, and then gently set them back down on their feet."

There's that look again. A couple students are intrigued by the parameters of the improv. Many look a little pale as they think about being responsible for carrying someone over their head across the room. A few people look almost hostile. They don't feel comfortable letting someone else take their weight.

I start the music and the dancers begin moving. This is the easy part. They all move for a long time while exchanging very awkward expressions. *Will you be the first to try? No? What about you?* The nonverbal communication that's happening is hilarious. It's like an awkward first date and nobody is willing to break the silence.

Finally, a brave soul makes the move.

"Me!"

She claims her presence loudly and then timidly begins her descent to the ground, wondering if the class will get to her before she collapses completely. They do. Almost effortlessly, they pick her up. The look of surprise on everyone's face is priceless. *Hey! She's as light as feather!* When you have twenty people hoisting up one person it becomes quite easy. The dancer lets go of all inhibition as she rides the wave of volunteering hands. She continues dancing in the sky until she is safely, slowly, and most gingerly placed back on the earth.

It doesn't take long for the next person to try. "Me!" Again, the class is buoyed up by the pure fun of the experience. Up and then down. Quiet laughter, lots of smiles, and a return to their own dancing world. "Me!" *Let's go again.* "Me!" We have two people who need help. Instinctively, the group divides and conquers to make sure no one is left to fall on their own.

One by one all the students take their turn. They are sensitive to the whole group, gently eyeing each other to ensure not too many people go at once. It's a simple lesson in give and take. It's a powerful lesson in being present. The non-verbal exchanges continue as each student silently surveys who has gone and who still needs a turn.

And then there's one. It happens almost every time I've guided this experience. There is one dancer who still isn't sure *she* will be fully supported. Often it is the student who feels she doesn't fit the 'dancer body' mold. She may have a little more weight to her frame than her fellow pixie-like peers. She doesn't want to burden the others with her perceived weakness.

Every time we get to the final dancer I hold my breath. My heart is quietly bursting. My first time participating in this improvisation was as a student several years back. I was that last dancer, and I didn't take my turn. I still regret it.

The class is gently prodding her with their gaze. *It's your turn,* they are saying with their looks. I wait to see if she's willing or not. She hesitantly but firmly says, "Me!" The class senses her hesitation and are more eager to get to her side and gently raise her up with ease.

The unspoken care for this person is a rare sight in our world of self-absorption. They take their time to carry her weight. The support offered is a whole new experience for this dancer who generally doesn't get a lot of practice in partnering and lifts. She closes her eyes and surrenders a little more to the trusting community around her.

They put her down. The music fades and is turned off. Everyone is silent. Hearts and minds are full of what was just experienced: Simple but profound lessons in trust, giving, receiving, and community.

Our Lost Tribes

The idea of community is often an unspoken principle in improvisation. We talk about trusting the process and our fellow improvisers. We have guidelines to keep us from saying "no" to our partners and being open to the ideas and interactions of others. We practice being present and available to the people we are working with. In fact, the most commonly taught principles of improv all connect to this very essential idea of community.

Our world seems in crisis as people feel increasingly isolated and disconnected from their own neighbors. The pace of society is quickening at an alarming rate. Our schedules are overbooked. Technology pulls us further apart. The news is always shoving the worst of mankind in our faces. Throw in the frequency by which we change jobs, homes, and careers and is it any wonder that the idea of community is dwindling?

What are the consequences of losing community? Beyond the obvious feelings of isolation, loneliness, and depression that occur on a personal level, there is also the breakdown within society itself. Studies have shown that lack of community and the resulting detachment from others increases violence, substance abuse, mental illness and more (8).

Committing to the idea of community, on the other hand, offers life and growth. Jean Vanier said, "Community is a sign that love is possible in a materialistic world where people so often either ignore or fight each other. It is a sign that we don't need a lot of money to be happy—in fact, the opposite (9)."

A healthy community is very much like a living organism. Individuals bring their own unique voice and strength to the group which, in turn, strengthens the whole. If one suffers, all suffer. When one succeeds, all succeed. When there is mistrust, all can feel it. When there is compassion, all partake. True community offers a vision of the interconnected nature of life.

In his thought-provoking book, *The Biology of Belief*, trained cell biologist Dr. Bruce H. Lipton challenges the Darwinian theory of "survival of the fittest." In his own words:

> "Evolution is a reflection of cooperation. Evolution isn't one animal against another—it's animals learning how to live in harmony with each other. Maintaining our belief in a Darwinian struggle of survival of the fittest is totally counterproductive to our actual evolution. And its destructive consequences of this belief of survival as a perceived struggle are responsible for most of the problems that we have on the planet today" (10).

How often do we consider our need for community as an essential element in our ability to thrive? We tend to get so caught up in 'me' and 'my dreams, my goals, my life' that we forget a very fundamental principle in life: *We are all connected.*

Improvisation taught me that real community is more than just casual interactions among people in close proximity. Sure, that may be where you have to begin, but true community happens when there is give and take; when you trust and are trustworthy. Communities listen. They witness. They care.

Finding *Your* Community

Consider the communities in your life. Family, friends, neighbors, and co-workers are obvious places to start looking. Keep in mind that community doesn't just happen. We must make a conscious effort to engage. We must actively seek to create an environment that allows all within to flourish. That's true whether you are looking to strengthen a neighborhood, a friendship, or a marriage. Real community takes effort. Finding a community of like-minded, like-motivated, and supportive individuals goes a long way in helping everyone achieve their goals.

What if you don't feel connected to any real community? How do you begin to create a safe haven of people who are truly invested in one another? Maybe

114

there are possibilities for community within the relationships you already have. Maybe you need to expand your parameters to include more people. Community is often defined by proximity, but it doesn't have to be. One of the benefits of our technological world is the ability to connect with like-minded people all across the globe. No matter how tight niche your interests may be, technology has made it possible for us to find people on common grounds. These relationships can be priceless. I do recommend, however, trying to find some real-life connections in addition to any online ones. There will be times when those face-to-face human interactions will prove to be critically beneficial and priceless catalysts for true happiness.

Planting the Seeds

Whether you are trying to nourish old connections or develop brand new communities, consider some of the following questions as you try to strengthen each one. The answers to these questions don't necessarily have to be "yes" for it to be a good fit, but if the answer is "no" be sure you understand the possible complications. The "no" answers can make things a bit more difficult in creating a harmonizing environment, but that doesn't mean they may not be worth it.

Do you share the same basic beliefs? While we should love and show kindness to all, when you are looking for a community that will help you progress it's useful to find people who have the same basic beliefs as you. I think it's wise to have many friends with many different viewpoints, but it's easier to feel more supported if your most closely-held values are shared or, at the very least, highly respected and understood.

Can you converse easily? Conversation is such a wonderful spark for feeling connected and creating new ideas. If you leave a conversation ignited, motivated, or simply feeling that you were really heard then stay with it. If the conversation always gets bogged down by negativity or someone always ends up talking about the weather, it may be time to try to pump new life into the discussion or move on.

Is the relationship equally shared in give and take? There are going to be times in our lives when we give more and when we need to take more. That's perfectly natural. But if you're in a relationship that is consistently one-sided you may need to ask why. The healthiest relationships are ones where both parties give a little and take a little.

As you ask these questions about the people in your life, you don't necessarily need to dump anyone on the side of the road if the answers don't seem to add up for you. Rather, use the questions as an opportunity to work on the relationship. All of our relationships can use some work. Building a community is very rarely a matter of luck. It's a seed that must be sown and nourished.

(Please note: If you are in an abusive relationship of any kind, please do not rationalize your way into complacency. Certain toxic relationships should be severed. Don't be afraid to reach out for help either from a trusted friend or professional.)

Beyond the obvious communities that naturally form due to proximity, other opportunities for community are all around. Consider your interests and passions and check your local community college for classes that might connect you with like-minded friends. Throw a neighborhood party and get to know the people you live by. Volunteer at community events and service projects to find people who are already committed to the value of community. You'll most likely find that you have many communities within your life such as your familial community, your neighborhood community, and the communities created from your work or interests. Honor each one for what they offer and make sure you are doing your part to nourish each environment.

Above all, you must put yourself out there. You must be willing to give. Be proactive about reaching out and breaking the ice. It may be uncomfortable, but you've already committed to risking so jump in and have fun!

ROBIN KONIE

PRINCIPLE EIGHT
create, adapt, repeat

"IN THE LONG RUN we shape our lives, and we shape ourselves. The process never ends until we die. And the choices we make are ultimately our own responsibility."

ELEANOR ROOSEVELT

WHEN WE THINK ABOUT creative individuals our mind usually tends to drift toward those with a talent for producing some sort of consumable artifact. The painter who creates paintings. The musician who plays a sonata. The seamstress and her beautiful clothing. The architect and his building.

The truth is, however, that we are *all* creative. "Creativity is a phenomenon whereby something new and in some way valuable is created" (11). Whether you feel creative or not, each of us are creating something new (and extremely valuable) every day: Our lives.

Most people don't often think about their life as a creative endeavor, but it's true. Our lives are the grounds for continual creation. Unlike the artist who starts with a blank canvas, however, our lives are anything but 'blank'.

We like to pretend otherwise. How often do we open our eyes and say, "Today is a new day. The slate is clean. I can be anything I want!" While part of the sentiment is accurate in that each new moment is an opportunity to consciously make anew, we will always be connected to our past, the environment, the people around us, and those things that make us uniquely us.

We are many things. Blank is not one of them.

That idea may turn some people off, but there is tremendous opportunity for greatness *because* of this fact.

Do the Opposite

Improvisation was always my favorite class, both in my undergraduate and graduate studies. One particular day during graduate school, however, I was just feeling worn down and ready to call it a day. I remember walking into the studio, hoping we would have an 'easy' assignment for the next hour and a half.

At first I thought I was going to get my wish. My professor had us take our place on the floor and instructed us to move however we wanted. "Let your movement reflect how you're feeling right now." *Perfect*, I thought. *I'm going to move slow, easy, and with minimal effort.*

For a minute we got to meander in this way. I indulged in the relaxed movement motif I had chosen. Life was good. Then I heard my professor's loud, commanding voice: "Now do the opposite!"

Seriously? Being the ever diligent student who was committed to getting perfect grades, I immediately switched gears and began dancing with intense, explosive, jarring movement. I hated it. I was ready to stop. But after about thirty seconds I began getting in a groove. *Maybe this isn't so bad.* I was feeling confident and pumped up from the dance I was creating in the moment.

"Do the opposite again!"

Like a car slamming on the brakes, my body jolted as my mind calculated what I was currently doing and what would be "the opposite." My initial reaction was that I should go back to my first movement motif. Logically, if the second set of movement was the opposite of the first it would stand to reason that the third would mirror how I started, right? But the process didn't seem so black and white. In the process of analyzing the movement I discovered many shades of gray and nuance that allowed me to better gauge what "the opposite" meant for me.

I began exploring circles. Circular pathways, circular motions, circular gestures. It seemed like the perfect contrast to the jagged, linear movement that I was just doing.

"Do the opposite again."

This time my movement became quick, short, small. Almost like my body was typing away at a keyboard. Nothing like what I was just doing, and still nothing like the explosive movement that came before.

We continued in this manner for quite some time. When it was over I was sweaty and energized. I was also completely surprised by how enjoyable the experience was despite the fact that it was pretty much *the opposite* of how I had hoped we would spend our time in class.

That experience was a reminder about the complex reality of life. We will find ourselves many times forced to "do the opposite" or change our course right as we are feeling in the groove. Sometimes those changes will provide relief; other times they will feel jarring and unwelcome. We can choose to feel victimized by those experiences, or energized by the fact that, no matter what comes our way, we still are the master creators of our world.

Are you willing to improvise the life you want? Are you committed to playing with everything the world throws at you to see what kind of masterpiece you can create? It's *the* great challenge of living. And it can be a lot of fun! The principles discussed so far will provide a framework by which you can deal with the complex nature of our world and still feel in control of your own dreams, but only if you incorporate the final principle:

Create, Adapt, Repeat.

You've considered your intentions, set your parameters, are ready to jump in, play, and suspend judgment while you take in the possibilities. Risks are inevitable, but you see them as opportunities to grow. You don't dwindle in past fears or try to live in the future.

You are present with an open mind. You are surrounded by a supportive community, and you care just as much for their success as your own. You are ready to create.

So… What do you *do?*

That is the ultimate question. Depending on your story and your hopes, it may be different than what your neighbor is going to do. Your first step may be as simple as a change in perspective. It may be as big as switching your career or committing to a relationship. I can't tell you *what* you need to do, but I can tell you this:

You need to *do* something.

Whether I'm choreographing a dance, painting a masterpiece, or building a house, there comes a time when **action** is required. You can't create without it. That action can come in many forms. It can come as words that need to be spoken. It can come in the form of physical hard labor. It can come by letting go of the things that are no longer serving you. Whatever that first step is, be willing to take it.

Begin creating. Now.

Create a Plan.

When I left my job as a university professor, my husband, Tom, was still self-employed as a die-hard entrepreneur—meaning: He wasn't making any money. Having grown up with parents who were both self-employed (and a father who was also always coming up with his next big business idea), I was comfortable with our situation. I knew our time would come when he'd realize the fruits of his labors. I wasn't worried about the fact that neither of us would be working for an unforeseen amount of time as we had prepared and planned well enough ahead that our savings would carry us through for a least a few months. Sure, there were times when one or both of us would silently freak out about our financial future, but, honestly, those few months while we both worked from home were some of the happiest memories of those first few years of marriage. We worked hard, even without a paycheck, because we were working on things we loved to do.

Not long after that we were expecting our first child. Tom's business was getting closer to launch, but we felt like it was time for a Plan B while we continued to get it ready. Thankfully, it wasn't long before Tom was able to get a job at a local company. What was even more wonderful is that the hours for this job made it possible for him to still be home in the morning to work on his own business.

We welcomed a beautiful baby girl into our home and life continued with Tom working his off-hours job. Slowly, however, the job started getting to him ... and me. Without going into all the details, suffice to say Tom was not happy in this job. At all.

At this point he felt stuck. His business still wasn't ready to bring in any income, but he was feeling worn out by a job that was sucking his joy away. I was home with a not-so-easy-but-totally-wonderful baby and felt stuck and unable to help him.

This could have been one of those moments where we just settled into routine and accepted that this is what life has to offer. *Maybe someday he'll get a promotion.* But was that really a comfort for our future? No. We knew a promotion wouldn't solve our problems because this job was not in line with Tom's intentions. Tom is an entrepreneur. His intentions have always been around building businesses he loves.

It's time to create, I thought. It was late one night, Tom was still at work, the baby was finally asleep, and I began brainstorming ideas to help our situation. Improvisation taught me that nothing is impossible. Sure, the forced parameters of our life seemed pretty restrictive, but I have always believed in the power of creativity.

With my trusty sketch pad and my favorite pen, I improvised a lot of ideas for our life and ways we could change the situation. Some of them were ridiculous (*move into a yurt and cut our expenses in half*) and others were less so. When Tom walked home that night I boldly declared my new intention:

"I'm going to earn enough money blogging so you can quit your job."

Tom looked at me with a warm smile. I could tell by the look on his face that he didn't believe me. He loved me and my willingness to change our situation, but he didn't believe me. His look didn't deter me from my intent. My little 'hobby' blog was already more than a year old and *maybe* saw a couple of visits a week from former dance students. I had never seen a dime from it. I had no idea how to monetize a website. But I was open to learning and working.

Before I knew it I was working my way through the first seven principles of improvisation.

I set my intention: To make enough money blogging so Tom could quit his job. I didn't mention a due date or an exact sum of money. I knew we had some flexibility in our style of living. I wasn't setting out to be a millionaire. We just needed enough to put us back in the driver's seat.

I recognized my parameters: I had to work from home. My baby was still my priority during the day. I didn't have any money to invest in this business.

I kept a playful attitude as I jumped in to the blogging world. I didn't want it to feel like work (although I was more than willing to work hard). I was passionate about what I was writing and wanted to keep the fun alive.

I suspended judgment for the first couple months as I doubled my efforts and waited for any return. I suspended my judgment when I would reaffirm my intentions to Tom only to see that "yeah right" look on his face. I wasn't going to let his doubts feed me.

I risked my time and myself as I poured hours into writing content, connecting through social media, learning about SEO, marketing, sales, working on an e-book, and putting myself out there for all the mean-spirited trolls. (Thankfully there were a lot of nice people, too.)

I practiced being present. The very nature of blogging can easily pull you away from the present and into a virtual-only world. I took time daily to meditate. I used yoga as a practice for being present and to stay connected to the world around me.

The community I found through blogging supported me in ways beyond my wildest dreams. I learned that there are no 'competitors' in the blogging world. It truly is a network of friends giving and taking.

So what about the final principle: **Create, Adapt, Repeat?**

This principle actually isn't the last step. *It's all the steps*. From the moment you create your intention you begin the process. You create, you adapt, you continue creating, you adapt some more, and you repeat these two simple steps while you practice the other seven principles. The process doesn't end (that's called *death*) but at some point you will realize that you are *living* the life you want. Right now.

8 months after I first declared my intention, my husband was able to leave his job for good.

It was amazing, but it wasn't a 'we made it to the finish line' moment. It was another chance to adapt to a new reality and continue creating a life we both love. We've had lots of opportunities for adapting and creating since that day. There have been plenty of halting 'do the opposite' moments that required major adaptations to our plan. Some of our experiences could easily be seen as failures or mistakes when pulled out from the bigger picture. But as we view life as a continual improvisation, we learn to honor those moments because we know how much we learn, grow, adapt, and utilize them to create something even better down the road.

Adapt. Always.

Stephen Hawking once said that "intelligence is the ability to adapt to change" (12). He's a pretty smart guy, but I'd still rephrase it just a bit to read: "Intelligence is the ability to adapt *with* change." It's subtle, but within that tiny word is the perspective that we are co-creating with the world around us. We don't just get knocked over and choose to stand back up. The very act of adapting is a creative process. It gives us a lot of power to be a force for good in the world.

Too many people fear change, or at the very least dislike it. But change is not only fundamental to every aspect of life (changing seasons, changing weather, change in movement), it is one of the most powerful tools by which we can create. You can't paint a masterpiece without changing the canvas. As you work through the first seven principles let this last principle keep you continually moving as life will certainly give you lots of opportunities to adapt, shift, change direction, go deeper, or create a whole new dream. It's what makes life rewarding and fun.

There is a kaleidoscope of colors and gradations filtering in from everything around us. Very rarely are things just black and white. Through the variations of life we realize our innate capacity for adaptation. It is in this ability to mold and accommodate that we find an ongoing catalyst for creation. As I said, we are not blank canvases just waiting to be filled with whatever color or image we desire. Instead, we come with a host of influences. The secret is realizing that those outside factors are the very tools provided to create a life we love.

CONCLUSION
the balanced life

"LIFE IS ABOUT taking what's given to us and creating something wonderful."

BELINDA JEFFREY

THERE ARE SOME PEOPLE who are bound and determined to set and achieve their goals *no matter what.* They make a plan, bury their heads, and get to work. These are the same people who are quick to remind others that not achieving results is an indication of too little discipline. These folks may work themselves to death, neglect relationships, or take on unhealthy habits all in the name of realizing a stagnant idea of success. We even share some of their stories for inspiration, usually leaving out the details about a life imbalanced.

At the other end of the spectrum are the individuals who think, *Life is what it is,* and give up by surrendering to their circumstances. They blame their finances, 'bad luck', or even other people for their lot in life. They've lost their creative force. They've settled for mediocre.

We are not victims of our circumstances any more than we are the chief commander of the universe. We are part of a synergistic environment, a connected world. When we let go of the 'do or die' mentality and incorporate the attitudes of improvisation, we realize that we aren't giving up on our dreams when we have to alter our plan. In fact, we recognize that life almost always forces us to switch things up. Instead of forcing results that isolate us from the world we live in, we expand our vision to adapt *with* life.

136

Set your intentions. Surround your daily living with the themes that keep you centered on your core values, hopes, and dreams. Recognize the parameters of your life and establish the guidelines that will help you dig a little deeper and find true freedom in the unique gifts you have to offer. Find the fun and enjoy the playful elements of life.

As you continue to suspend judgment, commit to the risks that keep you connected to your intentions, and are present with what life has to offer, you'll be more open to the communities and experiences that will provide growth and happiness.

Through all of it: Never forget your amazing capacity for creation. You are the creator of your life. Adapt with the forces that will mold your future and take action in developing a masterpiece beyond your wildest dreams. Be a force for good and help spark that creative flare in those around you. What are you waiting for? Jump in and join the dance.

POSTSCRIPT

Of the hundreds of improvisation experiences I've either participated in or led, none of them would have much significance if it weren't for the discussions and opportunities to reflect on the experiences afterward. Likewise, in our own lives we need to take a moment to reflect and make meaning from the pivotal moments. It's part of the creative process; a refining act for living a life we want.

Consider the experiences in your own life that stand out in your memory. What lessons do they hold? What can you learn from your mistakes or take with you from your successes? Share those experiences. Write about them. Talk through them with those who were involved. I believe everyone has a story to tell. We can learn so much from each other. Even more importantly, in the process of telling our own story we gain insights and perspective that provide fuel for our future.

REFERENCES

1. http://dictionary.reference.com/browse/goal
2. http://dictionary.reference.com/browse/parameter
3. *The Importance of Play in Promoting Healthy Child Development and Maintaining Strong Parent-Child Bonds* by Kenneth R. Ginsburg, MD, MSEd, and the Committee on Communications and the Committee on Psychosocial Aspects of Child and Family Health:
    http://www2.aap.org/pressroom/playfinal.pdf
4. Ken Robinson, "How Schools Kill Creativity"
    http://www.ted.com/talks/ken_robinson_says_sc hools_kill_creativity/transcript?language=en
5. http://sterlingscholar.blogs.deseretnews.com/abo ut/what-is-a-sterling-scholar/
6. *Yes, and... Improv Techniques to Make You a Better* by Lindsay Lavine:
    http://www.fastcompany.com/3024535/leadershi

p-now/yes-and-improv-techniques-to-make-you-
a-better-boss:

7. Babycakes Romero, *The Death of Conversation: I
   Photographed People Obsessed With Their Smartphones*
   http://www.boredpanda.com/the-death-of-conversation/

8. *The Importance of Community*
   https://www.washington.edu/admin/hr/benefits
   /publications/carelink/tipsheets/community.pdf

9. Jean Vanier, *Community And Growth*
   http://www.goodreads.com/work/quotes/25122
   64-la-communaut-lieu-de-pardon-et-de-la-f-te

10. *Interview with Bruce H Lipton:*
    http://www.soundstrue.com/shop/articles/Break
    ing_News-Science_Discovers_Intelligent_Life-
    In_Every_Cell-
    An_Interview_with_Bruce_H_Lipton_PhD

11. http://en.wikipedia.org/wiki/Creativity

12. http://www.brainyquote.com/quotes/quotes/s/st
    ephenhaw378304.html

ABOUT THE AUTHOR
ROBIN KONIE

Robin Konie is best described as 'eclectic.' Her driving passion in life is following her interests and creating opportunities from them. As a best-selling author, trained dancer, professional blogger, entrepreneur, 'retired' university professor, certified movement analyst, mother, and wife she is not afraid to mix things up and live her dreams fully. With an audience that has reached nearly 9 million people through www.thankyourbody.com, 4 other authored eBooks, and countless teaching opportunities, Robin has helped individuals around the world live healthier, happier, more fulfilled lives.

To learn more about Robin, visit her website:
www.robinkonie.com

Also by Robin Konie

The Clutter Trap: Learn how to organize your life for good!

All Natural Living: 75 non-toxic recipes for home & beauty

Processed Free: A real food guide to eating healthy

Live Pain Free: 60 somatic exercises to enhance mobility

and stop chronic pain